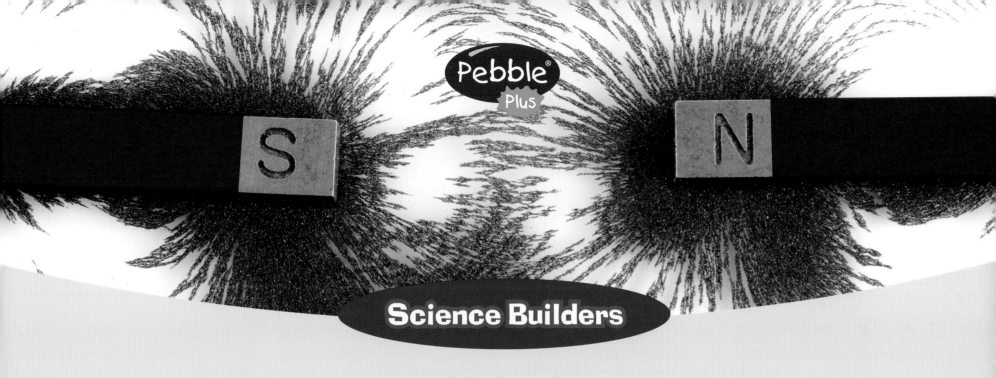

Pebble® Plus

Science Builders

A Look at Magnets

by Barbara Alpert

Consulting Editor: Gail Saunders-Smith, PhD

Consultant: Joanne K. Olson, PhD
Associate Professor, Science Education
Center for Excellence in Science & Mathematics Education
Iowa State University, Ames

DISCARDED

CAPSTONE PRESS
a capstone imprint

Pebble Plus is published by Capstone Press,
1710 Roe Crest Drive, North Mankato, Minnesota 56003.
www.capstonepub.com

Library of Congress Cataloging-in-Publication Data
Alpert, Barbara.
  A look at magnets / by Barbara Alpert.
    p. cm.—(Pebble plus. Science builders)
  Summary: "Simple text and full-color photographs provide a brief introduction to magnetism"—Provided by publisher.
  Includes bibliographical references and index.
  ISBN 978-1-4296-6069-3 (library binding)
  ISBN 978-1-4296-7109-5 (paperback)
  1. Magnets—Juvenile literature. 2. Magnetism—Juvenile literature. I. Title. II. Series.
  QC757.5.A47 2012
  538'.4—dc22   2010053932

Editorial Credits
Erika L. Shores, editor; Bobbie Nuytten and Ashlee Suker, designers; Wanda Winch, media researcher;
    Laura Manthe, production specialist

Photo Credits
All photos Capstone Studio/Karon Dubke except:
Shutterstock/Anton Balazh, 15, Levent Konuk, 19

Note to Parents and Teachers

The Science Builders series supports national science standards related to physical science.
This book describes and illustrates magnets. The images support early readers in understanding
the text. The repetition of words and phrases helps early readers learn new words. This book
also introduces early readers to subject-specific vocabulary words, which are defined in the
Glossary section. Early readers may need assistance to read some words and to use the Table of
Contents, Glossary, Read More, Internet Sites, and Index sections of the book.

Printed in the United States of America in Steven Point, Wisconsin.
072013   007586R

Table of Contents

What Is a Magnet?

What makes a paper clip jump?
A magnet! Magnets are made
of iron, nickel, or steel.

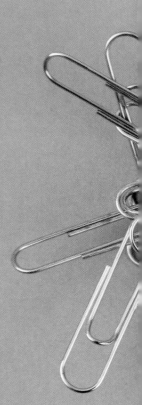

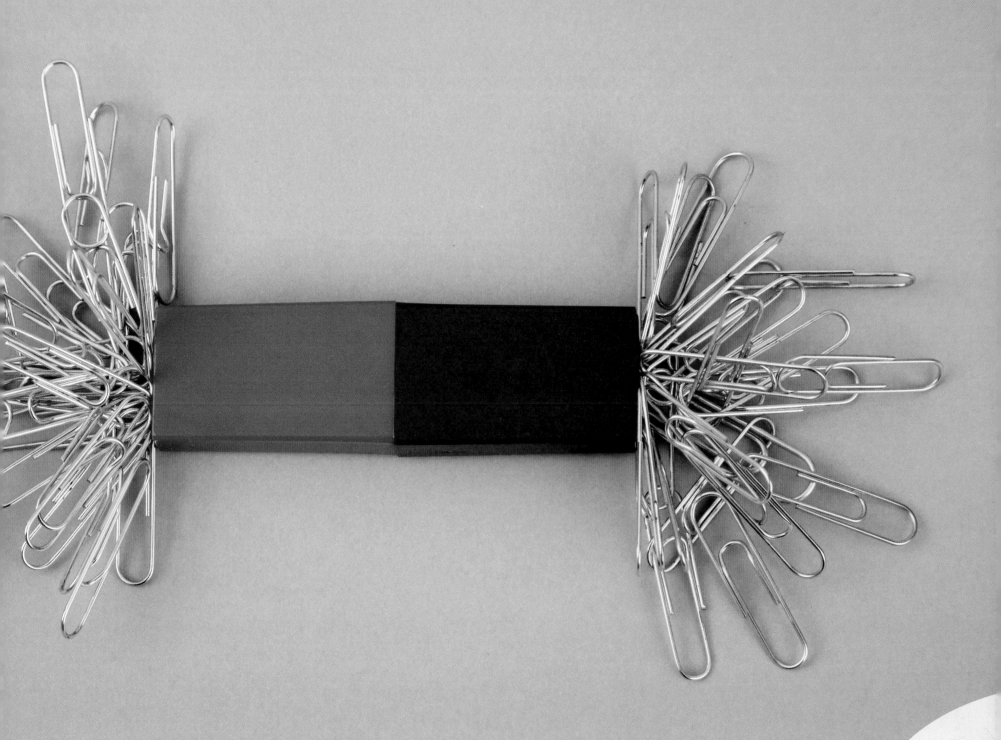

Magnets make some metal objects move. But magnets don't work on all metals. Can a magnet move an aluminum soda can? A copper penny?

How Magnets Work

An invisible area called
a magnetic field surrounds
a magnet. Iron filings show
the magnet's lines of energy.

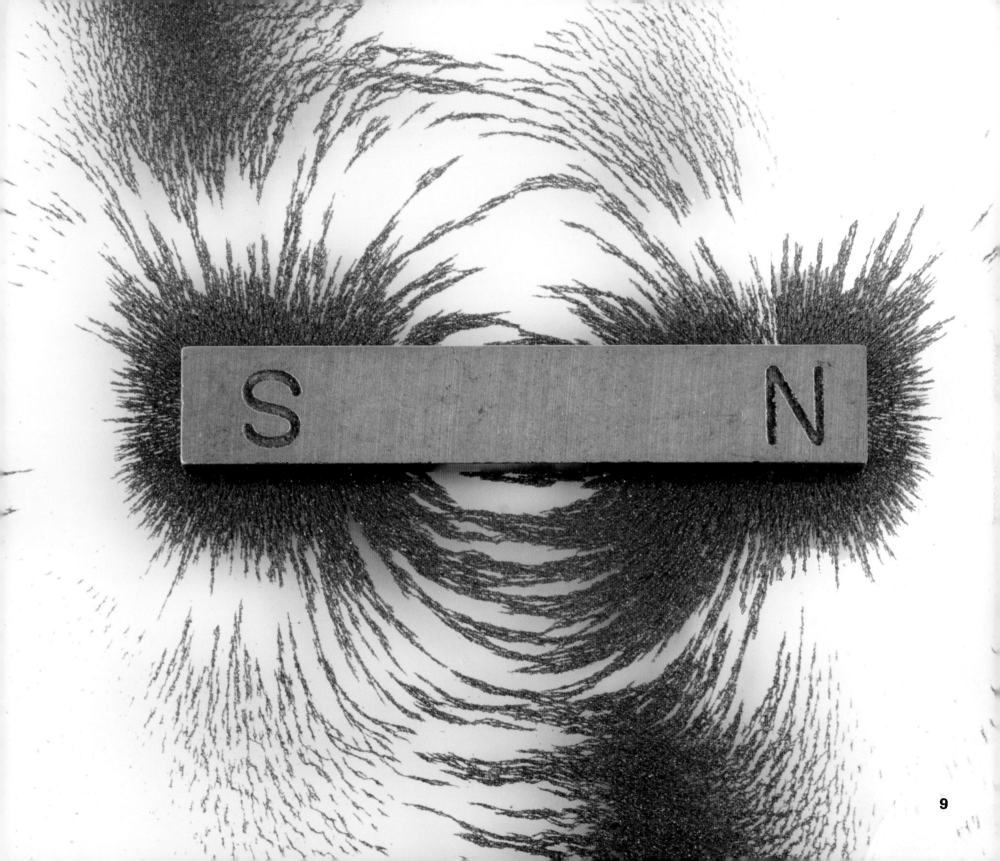

A magnet's pull is strongest at the spots with the most filings. These areas are called a magnet's poles. One end is north, and the other is south.

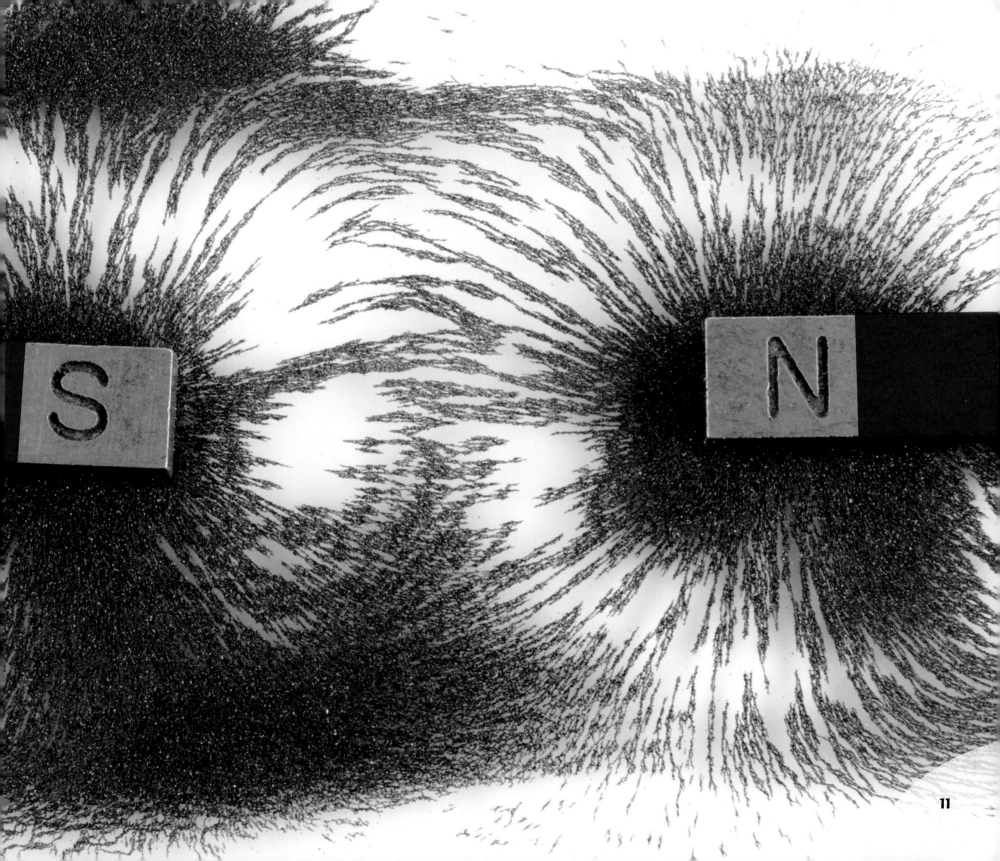

Try to make the north poles

of two magnets touch.

They will push away, or repel,

each other. But opposite poles

pull together, or attract.

Earth acts like a huge magnet.

It has a north pole

and a south pole.

North Pole

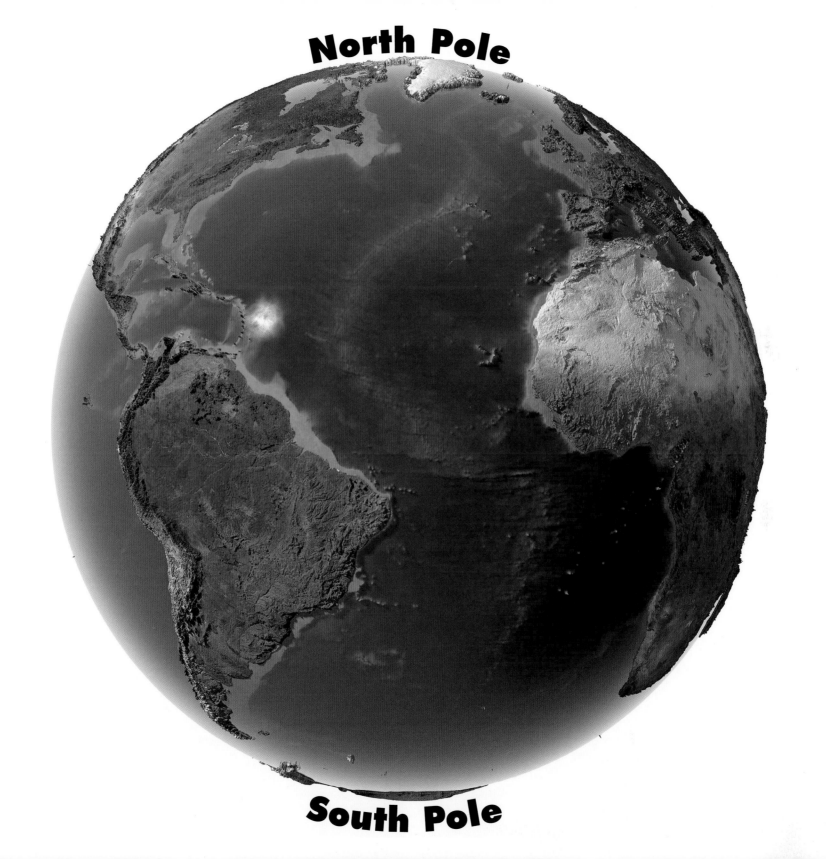

South Pole

Magnets at Work

Magnets show people where to go. A compass needle always points north. Earth's magnetic energy pulls it that way.

Magnets help doctors see where you are hurt. An MRI machine's powerful magnet helps make a picture of the inside of your body.

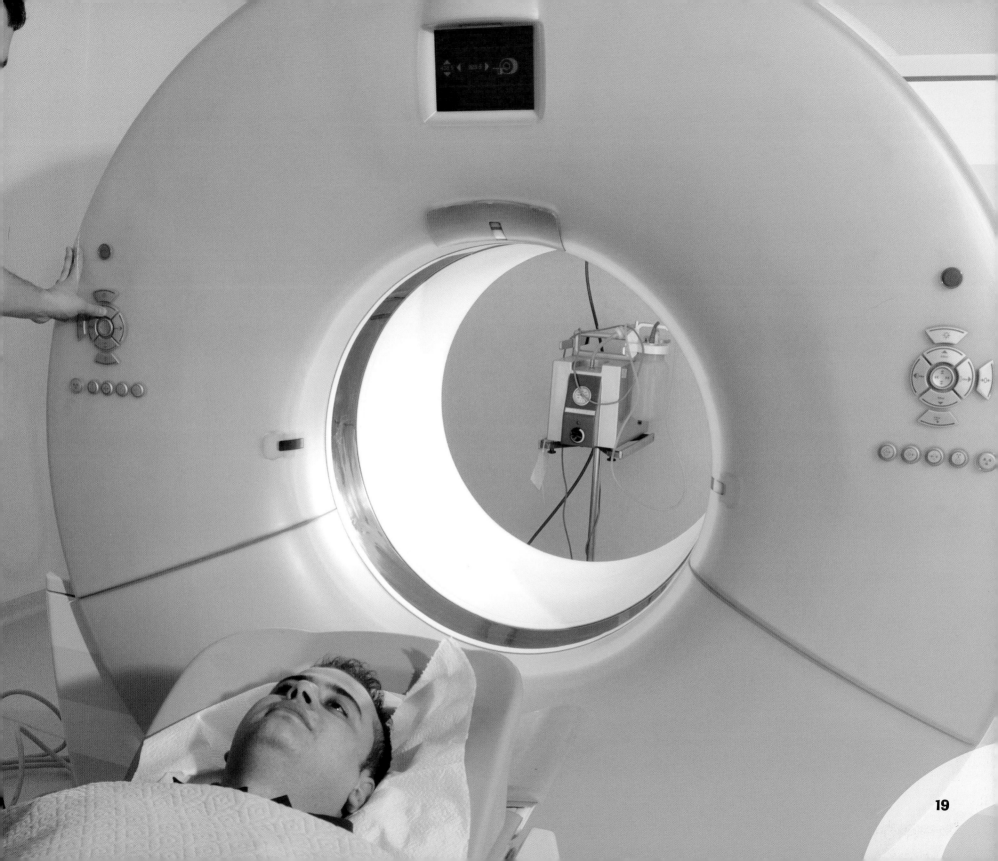

Magnets hold up pictures on a refrigerator. Credit cards use magnets to pay for what you buy. Magnets are at work everywhere you look!

Glossary

attract—to pull toward something

compass—an instrument used for finding directions

credit card—a small, plastic card used to pay for things; credit cards have a magnetic stripe on the back

energy—the ability to do work, such as move things

filing—a small piece that has been rubbed off of a larger piece

magnetic field—the area around a magnet that has the power to attract magnetic metals

MRI machine—a machine that uses a large ring magnet to make images of the inside of a person's body; MRI stands for magnetic resonance imaging

pole—one of the two ends of a magnet; a pole can also be the top or bottom part of a planet

repel—to push apart; like poles of magnets repel each other

Read More

McGregor, Harriet. *Magnets and Springs.* Sherlock Bones Looks at Physical Science. New York: Windmill Books, 2011.

Royston, Angela. *Magnets.* My World of Science. Chicago: Heinemann Library, 2008.

Vogel, Julia. *Push and Pull! Learn about Magnets.* Mankato, Minn.: Child's World, 2011.

Internet Sites

FactHound offers a safe, fun way to find Internet sites related to this book. All of the sites on FactHound have been researched by our staff.

Here's all you do:

Visit *www.facthound.com*

Type in this code: 9781429660693

Check out projects, games and lots more at
www.capstonekids.com

Index

Word Count: 192
Grade: 1
Early-Intervention Level: 22